Totline "Take-Home" Books
Alphabet &
Number Rhymes

Reproducible Pre-Reading Books
For Young Children

(Previously published as part of "Make & Take" Concept Rhymes.)

Written by Jean Warren • Illustrated by Cora Walker-Carleson

Editor: Gayle Bittinger
Layout and Cover Design: Kathy Jones

ISBN 0-911019-27-8

Printed in the United States of America
Published by: Warren Publishing House, Inc.
        P.O. Box 2250
        Everett, WA 98203

Contents

Alphabet Book

Farm Counting Book

Sea Life Counting Book

Introduction

Young children who are just becoming interested in books and reading are usually long on enthusiasm and short on ability. Totline "Take-Home" Books are designed to capture that enthusiasm.

Each pre-reading book centers around a particular learning concept and is written in rhyme. The unique feature of these rhymes is that young children are able to "read" them, using pictures as their guides. This happens because each rhyme is simply written and illustrated with pre-readers in mind. After reading a book with an adult a few times, your children will be able to "read" it by themselves.

Because all of the pre-reading books in this series are reproducible, your children can each have his or her own. And they will glow with pride and feelings of accomplishment as they take home their own books to "read" to their families.

General Directions

- Tear out the pages for the take-home book of your choice.
- Make one photocopy of the book for each child. Cut the pages in half.
- Place the pages on a table and let the children help collate them into books.
- Give each child two 5½- by 8-inch pieces of construction paper to use for book covers.
- Let the children decorate their book covers as desired or use one of the suggestions on the following pages.
- Help the children bind their books using a stapler or a hole punch and brass paper fasteners.

Suggestions for Using the
Alphabet & Number Rhymes
Take-Home Books

The take-home books in *Alphabet & Number Rhymes* are fun and easy to use. You can enlarge the pages to make big books for your room, introduce the rhymes with flannelboard cutouts, or give out books at the end of a unit about a particular letter or after counting and number practice. Following are some ideas for using the take-home books with preschoolers, kindergarteners and first and second graders. Mix and match the ideas to meet the needs and interests of your children.

Preschool

General Ideas
- Let the children use rubber stamps that correspond with the rhyme's subject to stamp the covers of their books.
- Give the children appropriate stickers to attach to the covers of their books.

Alphabet Book
- Cut the appropriate letter or letters out of newspapers. Let the children glue them to the covers of their books.
- Add extra pages to the end of each book. Cut out magazine pictures of objects whose names begin with the appropriate letter or letters. Have the children glue them to their extra pages. Ask them to name the items when they read their books.

Farm Counting Book
- Make paint pads by folding paper towels, putting them in shallow containers and pouring small amounts of paint on them. Give the children farm animal cookie cutters to dip into the paint and then press on their book covers.
- Have the children count the animals on each page as they read their books.
- Ask the children to make each animal's sound as it is named in the rhyme.

Sea Life Counting Book
- Have the children count the sea animals on each page as they read their books.

Kindergarten

General
- Have the children write their names on the backs of their books.

Alphabet Book
- Add extra lined pages to the back of each child's book. Have the children practice writing the appropriate letter or letters on those pages.

Farm Counting Book
- Have the children act out the story as you read it aloud.
- Draw barn shapes large enough to be book covers on pieces of red construction paper. Give the children the papers and let them cut out barn-shaped covers for their books.

Sea Life Counting Book
- Let the children act out the story as you read it aloud.

First and Second Grades

General
- Let the children take their books home to color.
- Have the children write "This book belongs to (child's name)" on their back covers.
- Have the children copy each sentence of a particular rhyme onto a separate page. Let them illustrate each of their pages.
- Photocopy each half page on a full sheet of paper with lines for writing below the picture. Have the children copy the words on the page.

Color Books
- Have the children cut out the appropriate letter or letters out of newspapers. Let them glue the letters to their covers.
- Attach extra lined pages to the backs of the books. Have the children practice writing the appropriate letter or letters on those pages.

Farm Counting Book
- Have the children cut out magazine pictures of farm animals and glue them to the covers of their books.
- Let the children make up new stories about where the animals went. For example, "One horse who lived on the farm, went out to the pasture for breakfast."
- Have the children write numbers on their book covers.

Sea Life Counting Book
- Let the children draw underwater scenes on their construction paper covers. Have them paint over their scenes with a blue tempera wash.

Alphabet Book

Aa

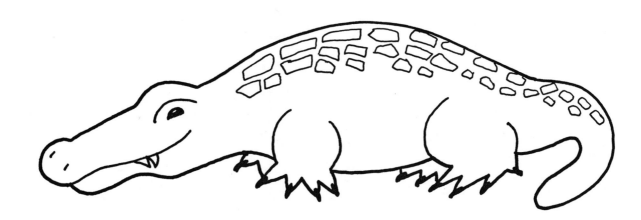

A is for alligator.

Aa

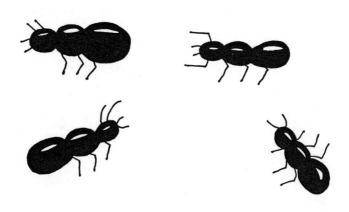

A is for ants.

Aa

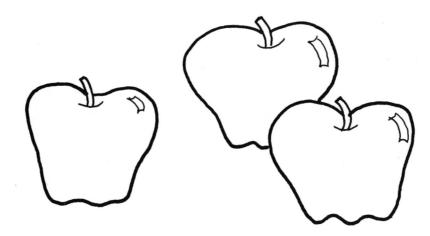

A is for apples

Aa

on my pants.

Bb

B is for bear.

Bb

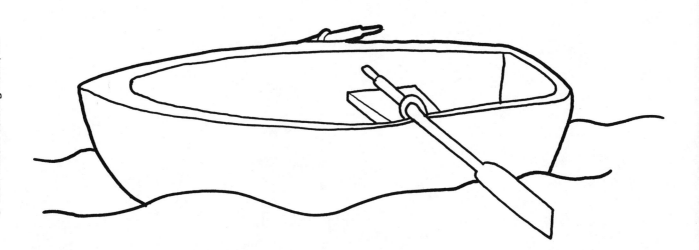

B is for boat.

Bb

B is for buttons

Bb

on my coat.

Cc

C is for cow.

Cc

C is for cat.

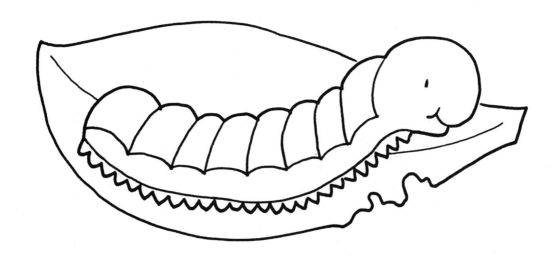

C is for caterpillar

on my hat.

D is for dinosaur.

D is for dog.

Dd

D is for doll

Dd

on my log.

Ee

E is for envelope.

Ee

E is for eggs.

Ee

E is for elephant

Ee

on my legs.

Ff

F is for fire engine.

Ff

F is for fish.

F f

F is for fox

F f

in my dish.

G is for girl.

G is for goat.

Gg

G is for gorilla

Gg

in my boat.

Hh

H is for horse.

Hh

H is for hair.

H is for hippopotamus

on my chair.

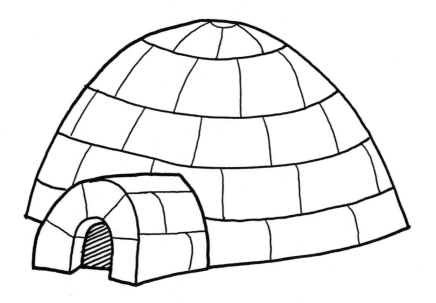

I is for igloo.

I is for ink.

Ii

I is for iguana

Ii

in my sink.

Jj

J is for jelly.

Jj

J is for jeep.

J is for jacket

on my sheep.

K is for kite.

Kk

K is for king.

Kk

K is for key

Kk

on my string.

Ll

L is for lion.

Ll

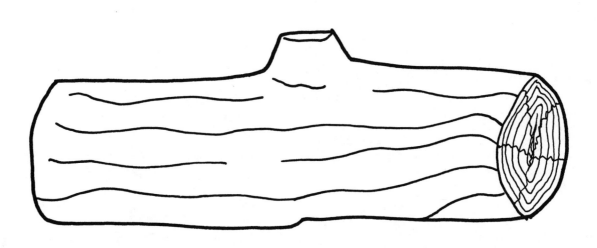

L is for log.

Ll

L is for leaves

Ll

on my frog.

Mm

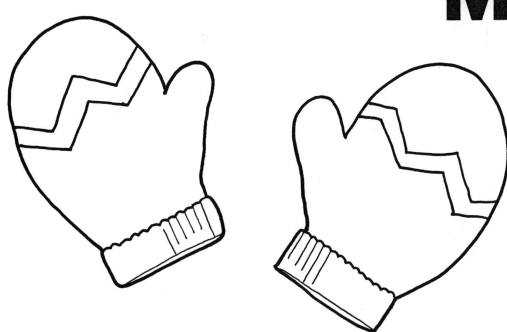

M is for mittens.

Mm

M is for mouse.

Mm

M is for monkeys

Mm

on my house.

Nn

N is for newspaper.

Nn

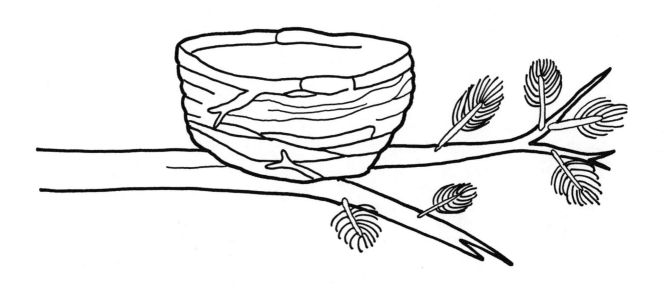

N is for nest.

Nn

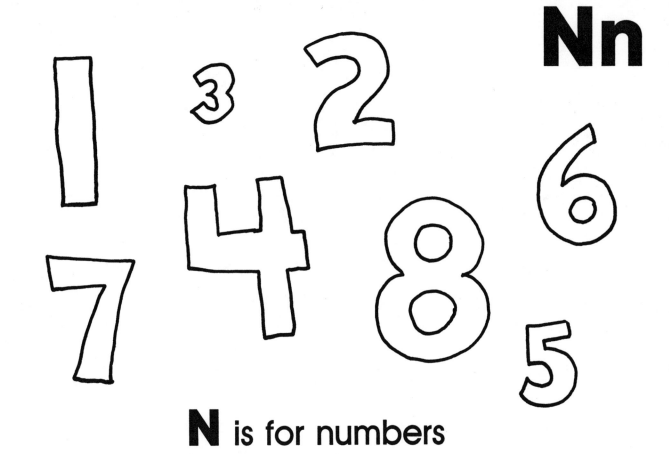

N is for numbers

Nn

on my vest.

O is for octopus.

O is for ox.

O is for ostrich

in my box.

Pp

P is for pizza.

Pp

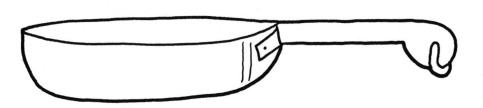

P is for pan.

Pp

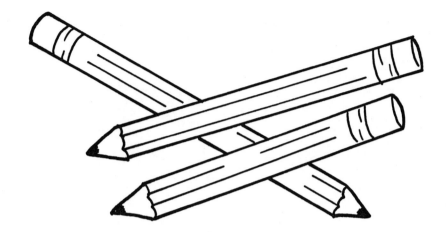

P is for pencils

Pp

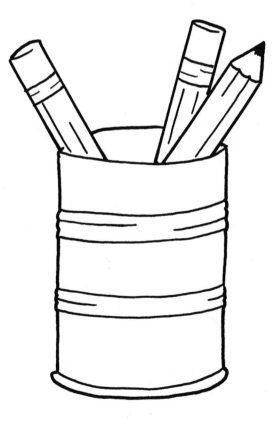

in my can.

Qq

Q is for queen.

Qq

Q is for quail.

Qq

Q is for quarters

Qq

in my pail.

Rr

R is for rose.

Rr

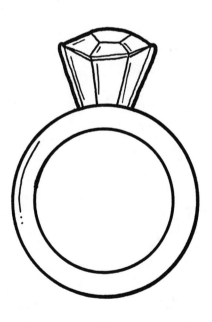

R is for ring.

Rr

R is for rabbit

Rr

on my swing.

Ss

S is for sun.

Ss

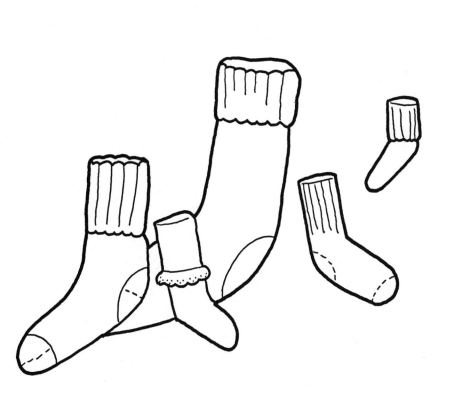

S is for socks.

Ss

S is for snails

Ss

on my blocks.

Tt

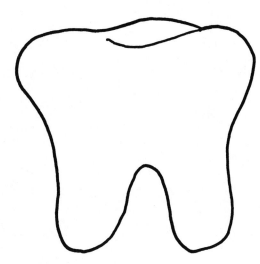

T is for tooth.

Tt

T is for truck.

Tt

T is for tie

Tt

on my duck.

Uu

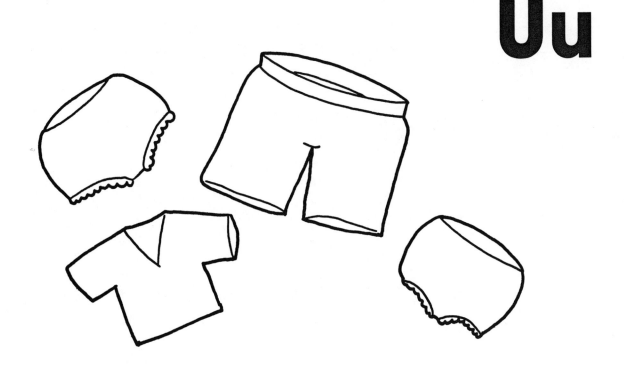

U is for underwear.

Uu

U is for up.

Uu

U is for umbrella

Uu

in my cup.

Vv

V is for violin.

Vv

V is for van.

Vv

V is for violets

Vv

in my pan.

Ww

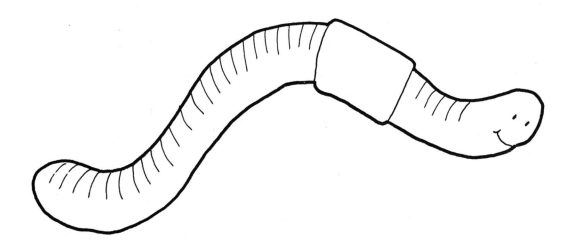

W is for worm.

Ww

W is for wagon.

Ww

W is for wings

 Ww

on my dragon.

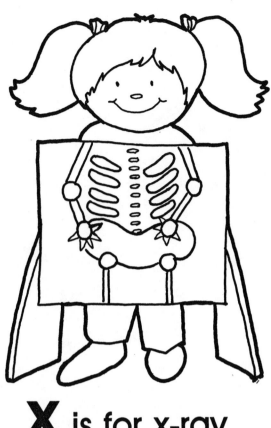

X is for x-ray.

X marks the spot.

X is for kisses

I have a lot.

Yy

Y is for yo-yo.

Y is for yak.

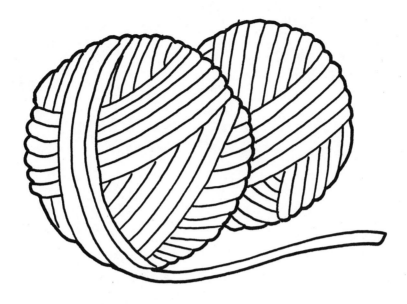

Y is for yarn

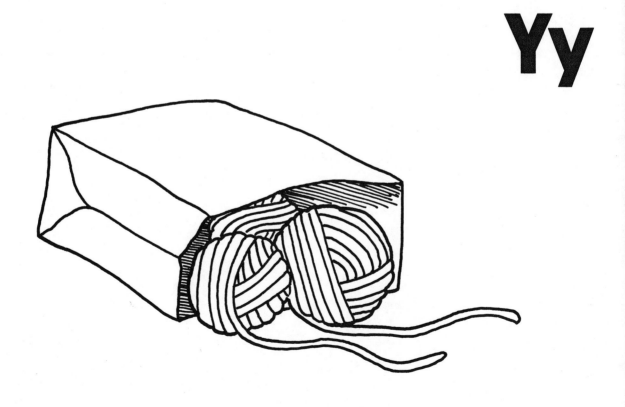

in my sack.

Zz

Z is for zebra.

Zz

Z is for zoo.

Zz

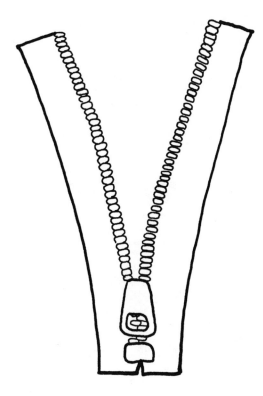

z is for zipper

Zz

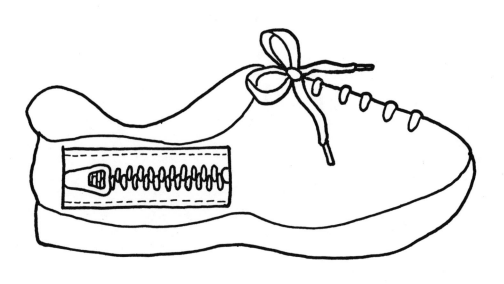

on my shoe.

Farm
Counting
Book

One horse who lived on the farm

went to bed in the big old barn.

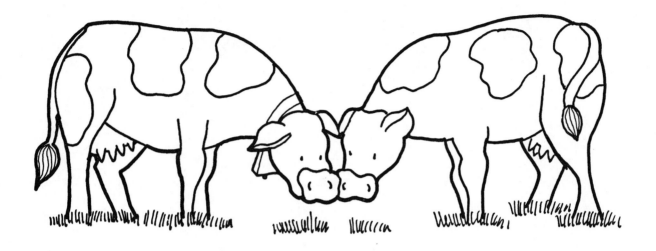

Two cows who lived on the farm

went to bed in the big old barn.

Three sheep who lived on the farm

went to bed in the big old barn.

Four goats who lived on the farm

went to bed in the big old barn.

Five pigs who lived on the farm

went to bed in the big old barn.

Six rabbits who lived on the farm

went to bed in the big old barn.

Seven ducks who lived on the farm

went to bed in the big old barn.

Eight dogs who lived on the farm

went to bed in the big old barn.

Nine cats who lived on the farm

went to bed in the big old barn.

Ten chicks who lived on the farm

went to bed in the big old barn.

Shhh!

Sea Life Counting Book

Ten little crabs who lived in the sea

jumped in the boat with Skipper and me.

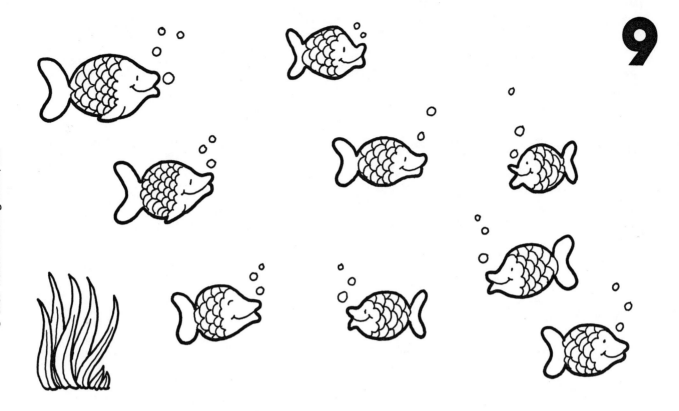

Nine little fish who lived in the sea

jumped in the boat with Skipper and me.

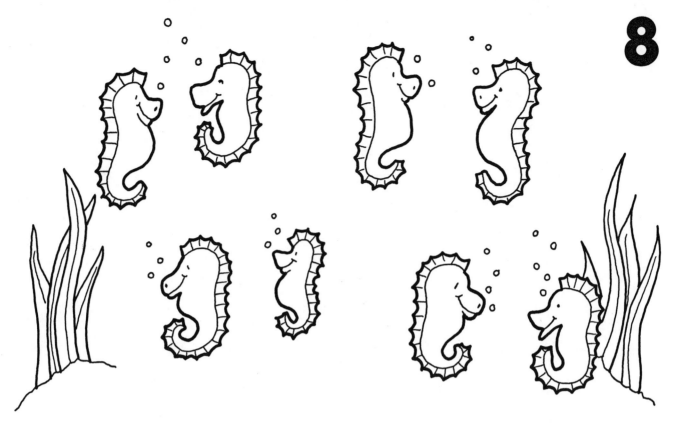

Eight little sea horses who lived in the sea

jumped in the boat with Skipper and me.

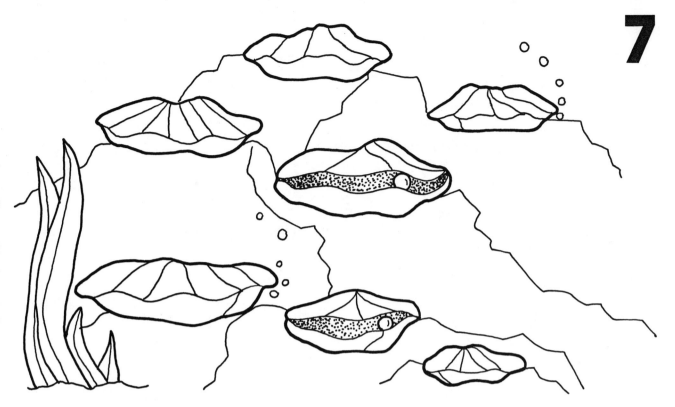

Seven little oysters who lived in the sea

jumped in the boat with Skipper and me.

6

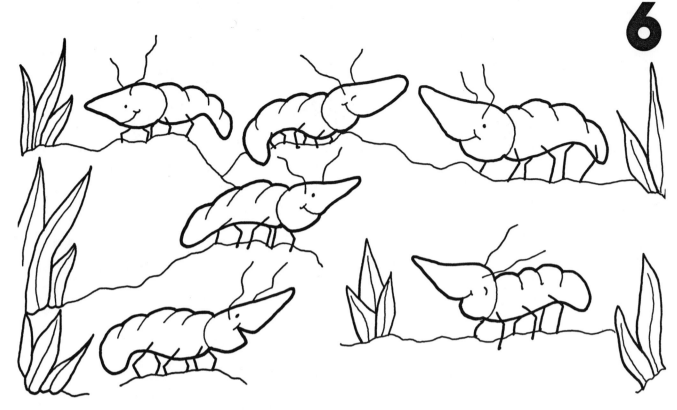

Six little shrimp who lived in the sea

jumped in the boat with Skipper and me.

Five little starfish who lived in the sea

jumped in the boat with Skipper and me.

Four little octopuses who lived in the sea

jumped in the boat with Skipper and me.

Three little sharks who lived in the sea

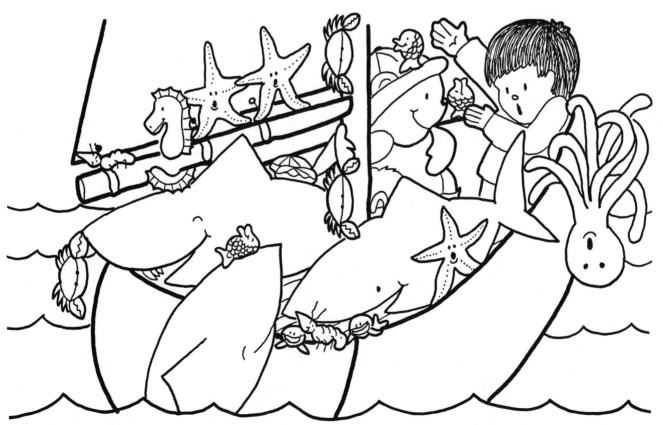

jumped in the boat with Skipper and me.

Two little seals who lived in the sea

jumped in the boat with Skipper and me.

One little whale who lived in the sea

Help!

jumped in the boat with Skipper and me.

Totline® Newsletter

Activities, songs and new ideas to use right now are waiting for you in every issue!

Each issue puts the fun into teaching with 32 pages of challenging and creative activities for young children. Included are open-ended art activities, learning games, music, language and science activities plus 8 reproducible pattern pages.

Published bi-monthly.

Sample issue - $2.00

Super Snack News

Nutritious snack ideas, related songs, rhymes and activities

- Teach young children health and nutrition through fun and creative activities.

- Use as a handout to involve parents in their children's education.

- Promote quality child care in the community with these handouts.

- Includes nutritious sugarless snacks, health tidbits, and developmentally appropriate activities.

- Includes CACFP information for most snacks.

Make up to:
200 COPIES per issue

Sample issue - $2.00

With each subscription you are given the right to:

Warren Publishing House, Inc. • P.O. Box 2250, Dept. Z • Everett, WA 98203

Totline® Books

PIGGYBACK® SONG SERIES

Piggyback® Songs

More Piggyback® Songs

Piggyback® Songs
for Infants and Toddlers

Piggyback® Songs
in Praise of God

Piggyback® Songs
in Praise of Jesus

Holiday Piggyback® Songs

Animal Piggyback® Songs

Piggyback® Songs for School

Piggyback® Songs to Sign

1•2•3 SERIES

1•2•3 Art

1•2•3 Games

1•2•3 Colors

1•2•3 Puppets

1•2•3 Murals

1•2•3 Books

1•2•3 Reading & Writing

1•2•3 Rhymes, Stories & Songs

1•2•3 Math

1•2•3 Science

EXPLORING SERIES

Exploring Sand

Exploring Water

Exploring Wood

CELEBRATION SERIES

Small World Celebrations

Special Day Celebrations

Yankee Doodle
Birthday Celebrations

Great Big Holiday Celebrations

CUT & TELL SERIES

Scissor Stories for Fall

Scissor Stories for Winter

Scissor Stories for Spring

TEACHING TALE SERIES

Teeny-Tiny Folktales

Short-Short Stories

Mini-Mini Musicals

THEME-A-SAURUS® SERIES

Theme-A-Saurus®

Theme-A-Saurus® II

Toddler Theme-A-Saurus®

Alphabet Theme-A-Saurus®

Nursery Rhyme
Theme-A-Saurus®

Storytime Theme-A-Saurus®

TAKE-HOME SERIES

Alphabet & Number Rhymes

Color, Shape & Season Rhymes

Object Rhymes

Animal Rhymes

LEARNING & CARING ABOUT SERIES

Our World

Our Selves

Our Town

MIX & MATCH PATTERNS

Animal Patterns

Everyday Patterns

Holiday Patterns

Nature Patterns

ABC SERIES

ABC Space

ABC Farm

ABC Zoo

ABC Circus

1001 SERIES

1001 Teaching Props

OTHER

Super Snacks

Celebrating Childhood

Home Activity Booklet

23 Hands-On Workshops

Totline books are available
at school supply stores
and parent/teacher stores,
or write for our free catalog.

Warren Publishing House, Inc. • P.O. Box 2250, Dept. B • Everett, WA 98203